A HAPPY FAMILY

APRIL 1942 AUGUST 1945

THE STORY OF THE
TWENTIETH INDIAN DIVISION

★

The Naval & Military Press Ltd

Published by

The Naval & Military Press Ltd
Unit 5 Riverside, Brambleside
Bellbrook Industrial Estate
Uckfield, East Sussex
TN22 1QQ England

Tel: +44 (0)1825 749494

www.naval-military-press.com

*In reprinting in facsimile from the original, any imperfections are inevitably reproduced
and the quality may fall short of modern type and cartographic standards.*

MONYWA TEMPLE: SEPOYS INSPECT ONE OF THE ORNATE BUDDHAS.

BATTLE OF IMPHAL, 1943-1944.

KABAW VALLEY - MOREH - BISHENPUR - NIPPON HILL - SHENAM -
MOMBI - PALEL - KYAUKCHAW - LITAN - IRIL VALLEY -
UKHRUL ROAD - CHINDWIN.

★

A HAPPY FAMILY

THE STORY OF THE
TWENTIETH INDIAN DIVISION

★

RECAPTURE OF BURMA, 1944-1945.

MAWLAIK - WAINGGYO - MAUKKADAW - BUDALIN - MONYWA -
AYADAW - MYINMU - NABET - IRRAWADDY (20 Div. Bridgehead) -
KYAUKSE - WUNDWIN - TAUNGDWINGYI - MAGWE-ALLANMYO -
PROME - KAMA - ZALON - LETPADAN - THARRAWADDY -
THONZE - TAIKKYI.

*Front cover photograph : Sub. Manbahadur Rai, 4/10 G. R.
with two Japanese swords he captured near Ye-U.*

FAMILIAR FACES :—

Brig. D.A.L. ("Long Mack") MACKENZIE, C.B.E., D.S.O., first Commander, 82 Brigade.

Brig. J.A.E. ("Jack") HIRST D.S.O., Commander Royal Artillery.

Brig. E.C.J. ("Jim") WOODFORD, C.B.E., D.S.O., second commander 32 Brigade.

Brig. S. ("Sam") GREEVES, C.B.E., D.S.O., M.C., first commander 80 Brigade.

Brig. D.E. ("Ted") TAUNTON, D.S.O., second commander 80 Brigade.

THE COMMANDER AND...

Maj.-Gen. D. D. GRACEY, C.B., C.B.E., M.C., Commander, 20th Indian Division.

... A FEW OTHERS

Brig. W.A.L. ("Jimmy") JAMES, D.S.O.,
first commander 100 Brigade.

Brig. C.H.B. ("Roddy") RODHAM, D.S.O.,
O.B.E., M.C., second commander 100 Brigade.

Maj. T.B.F. ("Tam") HUNTER, M.C.,
14/13 F.F. Rif.

Capt. A.N. FRADGLEY, R.E.,
of 481 Fd. Coy.

The VICTORIA CROSS

**Lt. A. G. HORWOOD, V.C., D.C.M.,
1 Northants,
January, 1944 (Posthumous)**

AT KYAUKCHAW during Jan. 18th, 19th and 20th, Lt. Horwood, Mortar officer, by great leadership when continually under fire, and by reconnoitring, guiding, and bringing up ammunition in addition to his duties at the Mortar O. P. contributed more than anything else to the success of attacks on a Japanese bunkered position.

On 18th Jan., he went with the forward company into action, and lay with his O. P. on a bare ridge throughout that day, shooting his own and other mortars while under intense fire. He returned with valuable information about the enemy. On 19th Jan. he directed fire in support of two more company attacks, and carried out a personal reconnaissance, drawing fire on himself.

He remained on the ridge during the night of 19th-20th, and in the morning shot his mortars again ; in the afternoon he personally led an attack with such calm resolute bravery that the enemy were reached. He was mortally wounded standing in the enemy wire.

**Jem. PARKASH SINGH, V. C.,
14/13 F. F. Rif.
February, 1945 (Posthumous)**

DURING the drive towards Mandalay a strong Jap force initiated a series of fierce attacks against Jem. Parkash Singh's position. He himself was wounded and ordered back to company headquarters, but when his Platoon Havildar and the officer commanding the platoon had also become casualties he crawled forward and took command. Propped up by his batman, he fired a two-inch mortar, the crew of which had been killed, and shouted encouragement to his men. When he had expended all the mortar ammunition, Jem. Parkash Singh crawled round the position collecting ammunition from the dead and wounded, which he distributed to his remaining troops. He was hit again while firing a Bren-gun and when he sustained a third wound, he lay down facing the enemy and continued to direct his men. Hit for the fourth time, he died shortly afterwards, telling his company commander not to worry about him as he could look after himself.

Summary of Approved Honours and Awards made to the Division up to August 1946

Award	Total for units of the Division	Total for units attached to the Division	Grand Total
V. C.	2	..	2
D. S. O.	24	1	25
Bar to D. S. O.	6	..	6
I. O. M.	18	..	18
M. C.	168	8	176
Bar to M. C.	9	..	9
D. F. C.	..	1	1
D. C. M.	7	..	7
I. D. S. M.	43	1	44
M. M.	231	9	240
Bar to M. M.	4	..	4
Total	512	20	532
Honour			
C. B.	1	..	1
C. B. E.	6	..	6
O. B. E.	13	..	13
M. B. E.	42	..	42
B. E. M.	4	..	4
Total	66	..	66
Grand Total	578	20	598

Certificates of gallantry 107

Mentions in Despatches 312

N.B.—Many Mentions in Despatches remain outstanding and are not included; nor are some awards for F. I. C. included above.

Units which served with the Division

ARTY
9 Fd Regt. R. A.
111 A-Tk Regt. R. A.
114 Fd Regt. R. A.
2 Ind Fd Regt. I. A.
22 Ind Mtn Regt. I. A.

ENGRS
92 Ind Fd Coy
422 Ind Fd Coy
481 Ind Fd Coy
322 Ind Fd Pk Coy

SIGS
20 Ind Div Signals

HQ 32 BDE

H. Q. 80 BDE.

H. Q. 100 BDE

INF.
1 Northants
1 Devons
2 Border
4-3 Madras Regt.
(replaced by 4/17 Dogra)
2-8 Punjab(Div. Recce Bn.)
9 M.G. Jat (M. G. Bn.)

9-12 FFR (Div. H. Q. Bn.)
14-13 F.F. Rif.
9-14 Punjab
4-17 Dogra
1-19 Hybad
5-19 Hybad
(replaced by 3/1 G. R.
1-1 G. R.
3-1 G. R.
4-2 G. R.
3-8 G. R.
4-10 G. R.
53 Coy "D" Force

S. T.
100 Ind G. T. Coy RIASC.
102 Ind G T Coy RIASC
175 Ind G T Coy RIASC
30 Ind A Tpt Coy
43 Ind A Tpt Coy
55 Ind A Tpt Coy
3 Ind Fd Amb Tpt
37 Ind Comp Pl
38 Ind Comp Pl
39 Ind Comp Pl
45 Ind Comp Pl

MED
42 Ind Fd Amb
55 Ind Fd Amb
59 Ind Fd Amb
10 Mob Surg Unit
26 Ind Fd Hyg Sec
56 Ind Dental Unit
70 Ind Dental Unit
25 Ind Mech Dental Unit
20 A M U

ORD
120 Ind Ord Sub Pk
10 Sal Unit

I.E.M.E.
63 Ind Inf Wksp Coy
64 Ind Inf Wksp Coy
20 Ind Div Rec Coy
134 Ind Inf Wksp Coy

VET
13 Ind Mob Vet Sec

PRO
20 Ind Div Pro Unit

INT
604 Ind F S Sec

POSTAL
76 F P O
120 F P O
122 F P O
123 F P O

ATTACHED

ARMOUR
7 Cav
11 Cav
150 R A C
3 D G
4-4 Bom Gren

ARTY
1 Med Regt
18 Fd Regt (S p)
10 Fd Regt
101 Hy AA
44 Lt AA

ENGRS
401 Fd Sqn

INF
Lifebuoy Flame Thrower Det.

INT
7 Pl B I C
11 Pl B I C

ISF
3 Sukhlet P

MISC
No. 1 Indep Bur Bky Sec.

CANTEENS
27 C B I D
40 I R S

ADDENDUM

(a) **DIVISIONAL UNITS**
   Under "ENGRS" add—309 Fd. Pk. Coy. R.I.E.
   Under "ST" add—127 Coy. R.I.A.S.C. Div. Tpt.
   75 Ind. AT Coy. (Mule).

(b) **ATTACHED UNITS**
   Under "ARMOUR" add— 3rd Carabiniers
   16 Light Cavalry.
   Under "ARTY" add—8 Med. Regt. R.A.
   Under "ENGRS" add—3 Engr. Bn. R.I.E.
   67 Fd. Coy. R.I.E.
   76 Fd. Coy. R.I.E.
   After "ENGRS" add—1 Ind. Inf.. Bde.
   48 Ind. Inf Bde.
   Under "INF." add—152 Para Bn.
   153 Para Bn.
   53 Para Bde. M.G. Coy.
   Kalibahadur Regt.
   After "INF." insert—R.I.A.S.C.
   14 AT Coy. (Mule).
   52 AT Coy. (Mule).
   MRD
   After "R.I.A.S.C." add—9 Mob. Surg. Unit.
   15 Mob. Surg. Unit

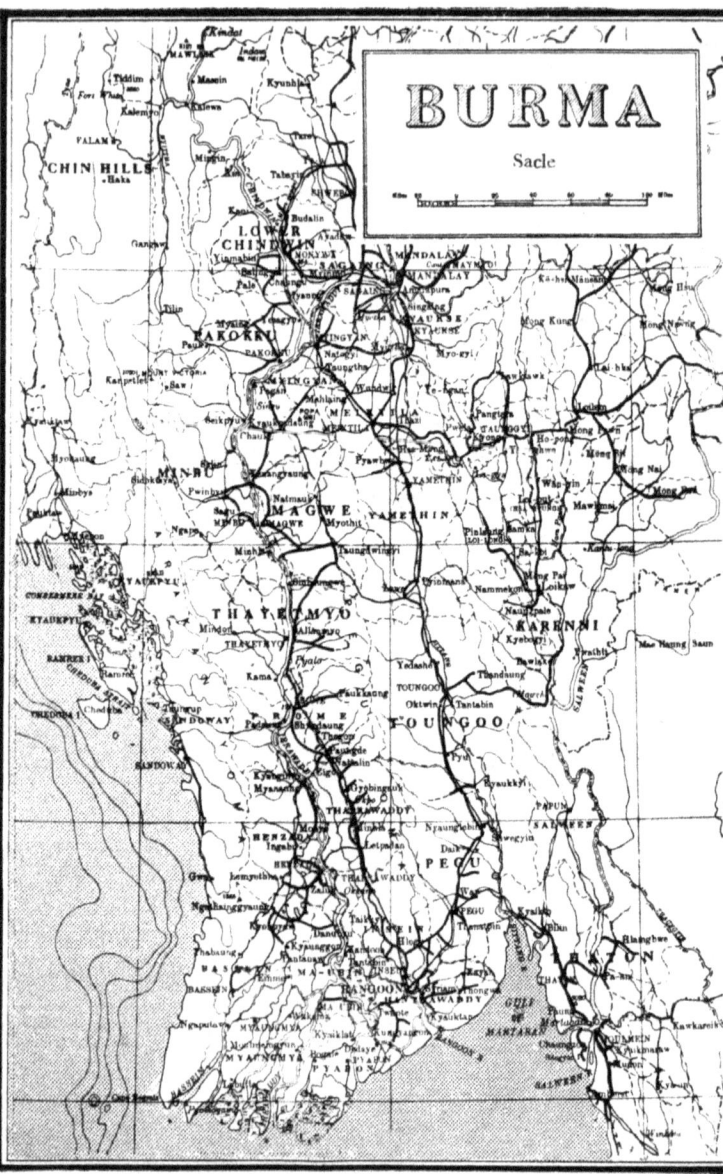

TROPHIES. Sub. Mahasher Lumba, Sub. Manbahadur Rai and Sub. Maj. Mansher Rai

A HAPPY FAMILY

THE FORGING OF THE BLADE

THE CURVED SILVER SWORD of Major General Douglas Gracey's 20th Indian Division has symbolised for the Imperial Armies of Japan swift and deadly execution.

For since the spring of 1944 when on the bloody heights of the Manipur Hills on the Palel-Tamu road the Division blocked the entry into the Imphal plain of the "Invade India" armies of Japan, until it reached the area Letpadan-Tharrawaddy-Hmawbi after a trek south-west from the Irrawaddy bridgehead at Myinmu where nearly 2,000 Japs alone were killed, this Division had wiped off the battle strength of the Japanese Army— practically a full Division of Infantry—killed and counted on the field of battle.

It was in the two decisive battles of the Burma War— the defence of the Imphal plain in the spring and early summer of 1944, and the breaching of the Irrawaddy Line almost a year later, that the Division's rate of killing reached its peak.

To what extent that unsparing slaughter broke the Japanese first in their vainglorious advance, and later in their fruitless defensive battle in Central Burma, the whole history of the Burma campaign bears witness. For the decisive factor ultimately in the defeat of the Japanese was the decimation of their infantry in successive suicidal battles in which they catastrophically matched their maniac audacity, against the determination to kill, of the Indian and British infantry of the Fourteenth Army.

The Division's reputation was founded on training—specific training for war in the jungle—and skill and hardihood acquired in battle.

General Douglas Gracey with 30 of his 31 years of service in the Indian Army, has been the only Commander of this Division. He commanded when it was raised in Bangalore in 1942, through its extensive training in jungle war in Ceylon, and throughout its active campaigning from late 1943 to the successful termination of the Burma war in the summer of 1945.

Characteristic of Gen. Gracey is his great personal concern for the welfare of his troops. The "jawan" he knows well—the Gurkha "sathi" even better, for he himself is from the 1st Gurkha Rifles, two battalions of which have won high honours in his own Division and during a pitched battle in the Irrawaddy valley, one went into action with the cry "*the General's Gurkhas charge!*"

THE TEMPERING OF THE BLADE

THE 20TH DIVISION was one of the few Indian Divisions in the Fourteenth Army which was trained solely for the war in Burma. The necessities of the war situation had made it imperative in the cases of most Divisions that they should be trained for service either in the west or the east, and jungle training came towards the end of their period of schooling when the call of the Mediterranean theatre became less imperative.

But General Gracey's Division under his watchful eye was schooled solely to beat the Jap at his own game, in his own kind of country. When it went into battle the 20th Division was like sharp and whetted steel. How keen it's cutting edge the Japanese were soon to discover.

THE TESTING OF THE BLADE

IN THE EARLY SPRING of 1944, when patrolling and brief actions on outpost lines was the general pattern of the war in Burma, the 20th Indian Division with its headquarters over the Indo-Burma Border in Tamu—the "village of the dead" of the Burma retreat of 1942—was prodding down through the jungle country to the banks of the Chindwin and beyond, and into the Kabaw valley seeking out the enemy, finding him and killing him.

The Division's order of battle then showed the classic constitution of an Indian Division—one British, one Gurkha and one Indian battalion to a brigade.

The British units were the 1st Bn. Northamptons, the 1st Bn. Devons and 2nd Bn. Borders; the Gurkhas—the 3/1st, the 3/8th and the 4/10th Gurkha Rifles; and the Indian Battalions—the 14/13th Frontier Force Rifles, the 9/12th Frontier Force Regt., the 9/14th Punjab, the MG Bn., 9th Jat Regt. and the 4/3rd Madras Regt.—the first Madras battalion in action in this war—as the Divisional defence battalion. The latter were later relieved by the 4/17th Dogra.

During those first few months these units put the lessons of their jungle training into practice and found themselves more than a match for the Jap.

These early days also brought a quick and brilliant honour to the Division—the award of a V.C. to one of its British battalions. Lt. Alan George Horwood, mortar officer of the Northamptons and already a winner of the D.C.M., secured the coveted award in a three-day action at Kyaukchaw which cost him his life. For two days he was a one-man O.P. for his mortars, in exposed positions and under constant fire. On the last day he led the final assault on the bunkers directing the attack from close range regardless of enemy fire. He was mortally wounded.

PARRY AND RIPOSTE

BUT THIS PERIOD of comparative idleness was not to last long. In the Arakan the Jap counter-offensive had been launched and beyond the Chindwin his divisions were preparing for the vaunted assault on Manipur to open the road to India and leave the Nipponese Rising Sun flying from the pinnacle of the Red Fort in Delhi.

With armoured elements as their spearhead, the leading Japanese columns crossed the Chindwin and made for the Tamu-Palel road which would lead them over the Chin Hills into the plains of Manipur and on to Imphal. Further west, invading forces were pressing up towards Tiddim against the 17th Indian Division which held the western outposts on the Tiddim road, and threatening an incursion into the plains of Assam in the direction of Silchar. Other forces were moving further north later to show a threat to Imphal from the east at Ukhrul and to get astride the Imphal road at Kohima.

The big Japanese offensive was on. Though in the Kabaw valley the 20th Division had attained early mastery over the enemy and everywhere held the initiative, the Fourteenth Army's plan made it imperative that they should withdraw. The entrances into the plain of Imphal were to be held. 4th Corps was to withdraw and form an iron ring around the southern half of the Imphal plain.

But the withdrawal was to be a fighting one—it was to hurry the Japanese as much as possible in their advance, and at the same time avoid getting caught by the tail.

With great skill the 20th Indian Division began to pull out. Men of the 12th Frontier Force Regt. harassing the Japs' Chindwin crossing inflicted large casualties. In the Kabaw valley at Witok, British and Indian infantry and gunners and tank crews had several field days against the enemy.

The first tank versus tank battle in Burma took place during this withdrawal. A party of the Border Regt. were lost after a Jap ambush, and British tanks were sent out to search for them. On the way they met a party of Japanese tanks and fought a swift engagement. Five Japanese tanks did not join in the march on Delhi.

At Moreh the 14th Punjab Regiment successfully ambushed the advancing enemy who often in blind confidence advanced in column of threes.

IMPHAL. Men of the 3rd Madras Regt. on patrol.

Even in the withdrawal the Division had started its slaughter of the enemy.

Westwards towards Palel, ribboned by the winding road which had first been built to extract General Alexander's army from Burma in 1942, lay the tangled mass of the Chin Hills, rugged broken country covered with scrub, with peaks rising to 5000 feet.

It was on this strange battlefield where deployment was difficult, if not impossible, where the single road axis could be commanded with ease by guns and infantry, and where war was to consist of entrenched garrisons with perimeters heavily wired and mined holding grimly to peak tops in face of shelling and suicidal attack, that the 20th Division was to make its stand. Supply of ammunition, food and water was a difficult but not unconquerable problem. The ground must be held—that was the fiat and General Gracey's men prepared to hold it.

At no stage during the withdrawal was the Division pressed to its limit. Successive actions were fought which delayed and took toll of the enemy before the pull out was made towards the vital ground beyond which the invaders must not pass.

On Shark feature the 3rd Madras Regt. signalised itself in battle by holding out against heavy enemy attacks and leaving many dead on its perimeter.

On Nippon Peak, the Devons after air strikes and artillery bombardment winkled the Japs out of their twenty foot deep entrenchments to regain the height. In this action practically the whole of the enemy garrison of the peak was wiped out.

On Sita ridge, the 1st Gurkhas after a two-hour artillery bombardment which lasted until dawn held out against wave after wave of attacks supported by medium machine guns, and killed 200 Japs including seven officers. A relief column on a fourteen miles march forward killed more on a road block and in patrol clashes.

The pattern of the Jap tactics was becoming clear. They were prepared to stake all on a break through and to throw wave after wave of suicidal infantry against our positions in an attempt to breach our perimeter.

On our side the pattern was clear too. We would hold to the last limit where we need not hold and hold to the very last where we had to hold.

The Colonel of the 1st Gurkhas after the Sita ridge action made a comment which summed up the attitude of the troops of the Division, *"The Japanese plan suits us well,"* he said, *"there is a nice interval between each wave in which our men can get up their ammunition and refill magazines. Then we are ready for the next lot"*.

SUMMIT of NIPPON PEAK captured by men of 1 Devons.

On the Shenam saddle, the surrounding features began to bear historic names. The map terminology for the whole area took its origin from the Mediterranean—Britain's stronghold in the war in the Middle East. "Crete", "Malta" and "Gibraltar" were three of the features—dominating the road. Another—"Scraggy"—gained its name from its appearance only. This tangle of peaks and ridges on each side of which stretched the blue distances of the Chin Hills and through which ran the hair-pin Tamu road, were to be Allied bastions.

The dispositions were completed in good order and in good time. The Divisional headquarters was on a hilltop near Palel where lay the airfield which the Japs proposed to capture. The whole of the southern ring of steel became largely a 20 Division responsibility.

One brigade was formed on the Shenam saddle, another was at Bishenpur on the Tiddim road under command of 17 Indian Division with elements of that Division guarding the Bishenpur-Silchar track, while a third which formed a reserve force and defended the airfield was located in the open country between the Tamu and the Tiddim roads.

While fighting of the greatest severity was centred on the Shenam saddle the other forces of the Division were by no means idle.

The brigade at Bishenpur, with its headquarters in a wood at the foot of the Silchar track, was shelled with unpleasant regularity by enemy long-range guns. The Japanese were massing to the south and the holding of the line necessitated tank supported forays against villages like Ningthoukong—later to be an important battlefield— which had to be carried out with limited artillery support.

Five thousand feet up on the Silchar track, on what was christened Hampton Hill, the Northamptons and 8th Gurkhas guarded the precious route which led to the plains of Assam.

Here a company of the British battalion with the 8th Gurkhas fought an incredible action at night in which tanks which had climbed 2,000 feet to the peak up a twisting corkscrew track, the last part of which was hewn out of solid bamboo jungle by Sappers, turned on their headlights to assist the defending Infantry. The suicidal attacks were beaten off and the track safeguarded.

Between the roads, a battalion of the 13th Frontier Force Rifles—whose Colonel later became a brigade commander in the 5th Indian Division—was "playing Pathan" over a 1,000 square miles of jungle from an advance base at Shuganu.

"Tiger patrols" of a handful of men strung with hand grenades and armed with a high proportion of automatic weapons went out into the jungle for days at a stretch carrying their own rations, living on the country, and moving by map and compass.

They ambushed Jap columns on their lines of communication and struck terror into the heart of the invader who by the widespread depredations of this tiny force of Indian soldiers became convinced that a body of a considerable size was poised for the defence of the Imphal plain in this area.

On the Shenam saddle the bitter battle went on. Though the enemy could not deploy his artillery he used it to its best effect by bringing down concentrations on our positions whenever they intended to attack.

" Brigade Hill," where in deep timber-baulked dugouts the staff stuck it out, was hammered nightly. Our own guns disposed in extraordinary fashion in bays along the winding road hammered back.

Off "Crete " a twenty-five pounder knocked out a Jap tank with a direct hit—and there it lay by the roadside a memorial to the futile use of armour by the invader.

On " Crete " the 1st Gurkhas showed the Japs a taste of their metal when they went over the top with flashing kukris in a counter-attack. " Scraggy " was another battlefield for the 1st Gurkhas, and their bravery here at one time saved the situation from becoming too harassing for comfort.

Sita ridge where they had fought a previous action was later known as " Malaun " in their honour, the 1st Gurkhas keing known as the " Malaun " Regiment after the Fort of that name near Sabathu in which the Gurkhas were finally defeated by the British and were allowed to march out with honours of war.

By this time the Tokio radio boosting civilian morale with accounts of false success, was claiming that the garrison in Imphal were eating rats, and that the march to India was on.

On one occasion it claimed the capture of Palel airfield. More succinctly a Divisional situation report summed up this minor incursion towards the vital airfield by stating " *the enemy are being slain now.*"

A brigade of the I. N. A. were given part of this task but the majority fell into the hands of our troops as prisoners or were killed in action.

In the defence of the airfield a prime task of the Division was preventing the Jap from bringing his guns forward to get within range of it. Patrols were constantly probing forward offensively north and south of the road and in one action in blinding rain caught an enemy concentration digging and preparing food. The remains of 200 Japs were found by a later patrol.

By now the Japanese offensive was coming to its bloodstained and catastrophic end, and the forces of the Fourteenth Army were being poised for the pursuit and annihilation which was to break the back of the Japanese Army in Burma.

The 20th Division in the southern line pulled out and counted the slaughter. Counting all sectors and reckoning the fighting from Tamu to the Shenam saddle, the Division in its first big engagement could reckon on having killed some 2,500 Japs. The sharpness of the sword had been felt on the neck of Nippon.

To the north operations were still going on along the Ukhrul road where the last of the Japanese force that attempted to reach Imphal from the east were being driven back towards the Chindwin and squeezed from the north by forces of the 7th Indian Division which had worked down from Kohima.

In the clearing up of this pocket the 20th Division played its part.

On the Ukhrul road 100 Brigade was holding the Saddle overlooking the Thoubal river towards Litan, but overlooked by the Japanese 51st Regt. on the "Sausage" feature to the north. With the breaking of the monsoon mechanised warfare was greatly limited, and even A. T. movement across country and on the minor tracks became very difficult. The Japanese position was thus very strong, while at the same time any encircling movement must have seemed to them impossible. 80 Brigade, however, achieved this, moving north up the Iril river valley by night to cut the enemy line of withdrawal from Kanglatongbi area, and

UKHRUL ROAD. Transport goes over temporary river crossing.

forcing the 51st Regt. to pull back the Battalion on its right flank. They then came down on two tracks, the Devons establishing a road block near Finches· Corner, the rest of the Brigade pushing the Japs back through Aishan towards 100 Brigade who had also made a smaller encircling move south of Litan.

The Japs during this period had made a last attempt to break into the Imphal plain and suffered heavy casualties. Now finding themselves trapped, they made a des-

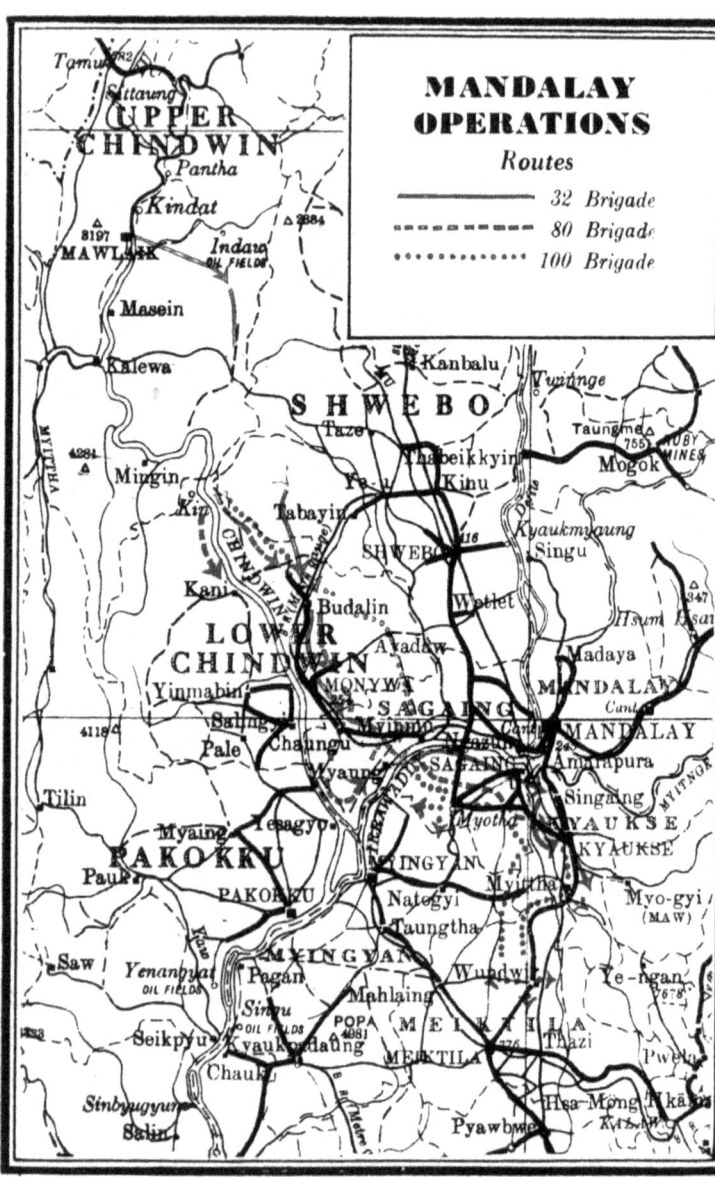

perate attempt to escape but were practically annihilated during a grim "pheasant shoot" conducted by the two brigades, which had linked up. The scattered remnants streaming back from Sangshak to Humine suffered another 500 casualties inflicted by troops of 153 Parachute Battalion operating under Divisional command.

The Imphal plain was now clear of the invader, the counter-thrust had been launched along the Tamu road from the Shenam saddle which General Gracey's men had held so stubbornly and decisively. The pursuit along the Tiddim road was beginning.

AN INTERLUDE.

THE 20TH DIVISION went into rest—but only to train for the next stage of the Burma War. They picked out the lessons of the past months and perfected their initial training. The sword went back on the grindstone for a new edge.

THE THRUST OF THE BLADE.

NOVEMBER OF 1944 saw them on the march again into their second spell of fighting. In common with other 14th Army troop the Division's objective was Mandalay, but with a difference.

The main function of the 20th Indian Division in the overall plan was to act as the right flank guard to the 14th Army troops committed to make a frontal attack on Mandalay.

After a few weeks spent in forming up, one of its brigades concentrated near the Burmese township Mawlaik which had been earlier cleared by an East African Division.

The plan was to cross the Chindwin river and then drive southwards through the arid, trackless hill country along the eastern bank of the river.

Foot-slogging troops of the 20th Indian Division became "expert sailors" while crossing the 600-yard span of the river, in craft ranging from the local "thanban"—a crudely shaped rowing boat—to hastily constructed rafts fitted with out-board motors. This was 14th Army's first bridgehead across the Chindwin.

In addition to about 5,000 men, and 1,350 mules the Division's Indian and British troops had to ferry across hundreds of tons of stores and equipment and mountain guns.

The first party set out on the 2nd of December and the whole move was completed by the 8th. Some of the 28 ranger-boats dropped by air were damaged on landing and the whole operation became a masterpiece of improvisation.

Mules proved to be the most difficult customers. They broke loose in mid-stream and had to be goaded back to the starting point. Another of their difficulties was the morning mist which necessitated accurate navigation with the compass to avoid sandbanks in the middle of the swift flowing river.

With hardly a dozen rubber boats and two rafts made out of empty drums which the engineers found lying about, on an average over 1,000 men and 300 mules were taken across daily.

Sterling work was done by men of the Bombay Sappers and Miners who built the rafts and "mechanised" the Burmese river-craft which made the crossing possible.

Hurriedly improvising a river-side workshop, Sikh, Punjabi Mussalman and Mahratta sappers immediately set to work. Besides dealing with current repairs they had to attend to the ranger-boats which had been damaged in transit and build the much-needed rafts from stray material.

They had to work night and day, almost non-stop. Often they were chest deep in water when the ropes supporting the out-board motors started to give way in midstream.

The crossing also was later the scene of a pwe—at which Indian and British servicemen played hosts to over 2,000 emaciated and misery-ridden Burmese villagers who had been forced to live a nomadic life in distant jungles. Many of these who had helped generously at the time of the crossing were personally thanked by the Divisional Commander.

With this move the Divisional plan of action began to unfold itself. While the Brigade across the Chindwin maintained its southwards push, the rest of the Division after a three days' dash concentrated further south on the eastern bank of the river, at Maukkadaw.

Since the first crossing, Kalemyo and Kalewa had fallen and a Bailey bridge had been thrown across the Chindwin, near Kalewa, which enabled General Gracey to bring the rest of his Division across.

The trans-Chindwin brigade maintained its progress against slight opposition but under many difficulties mainly caused by the absence of any roads worth the name; and supplies had to be air-dropped throughout the long march which finally ended at Budalin.

In the meantime the main interest centred round the bridgehead at Maukkadaw, which Gen. Gracey decided to use as a spring-board for another surprise appearance along the east bank of the Chindwin a few miles further south.

Owing to the nature of the country a straight push along the river bank was impossible. In order to reach their objective the Division had to cross the Chindwin twice—first from Maukkadaw to the western bank and then, after a short march, back to the eastern bank.

Having crossed the Chindwin for the last time, as the Division was preparing for a large-scale sweep along the western outskirts of the Shwebo plain unobstructed by any other river barrier till reaching the Irrawaddy, came the news of its long isolated brigade nearing Budalin—the largest town on the north-western edge of the Shwebo plain. They had encountered little opposition from the fast retreating enemy but already their bag of Jap dead was touching the 200 mark—top honours for the "kills" going to the men of a battalion of 10th Gurkha Rifles. One Gurkha platoon led by Subedar Mahabir Limbu, killed over 50 Japs, including two officers and a senior NCO, in an ambush near a causeway in the area of Pyingaing, north-west of Ye-U. The whole action lasted only a few minutes.

Shortly afterwards these Gurkhas, while clearing a stretch of road which the 2nd British Division was following into Ye-U, inflicted more havoc on the enemy. Subedar Manbahadur Rai personally captured two Jap Officers' swords, one of them after a hand-to-hand encounter with the owner.

The brigade had marched for nearly 250 miles in just six weeks, through mountain jungles where they had often to cut their own paths.

Completely surprising the enemy the brigade then appeared at the gates of Budalin. Holding the town was a Jap garrison with orders to fight to the last man.

Fierce fighting raged for over a week. Men of the Northamptonshire Regiment, as spearhead of the attack, inflicted severe casualties on the enemy. Out of the total Jap force of well over a hundred only 10-15 Japs escaped alive.

Working yard by yard the troops of the 20th Indian Division first occupied the main road junction and then started tightening their ring on the enemy till they were squeezed into a small pocket.

During the attack the troops had to reckon with over six strongly built defensive positions and hundreds of dugouts which were used by enemy snipers. All through the action the men had to advance over flat country which was covered with well sited Jap machine guns.

In this battle—the first to be fought by the 20th Indian Division in 1945—the Northamptons were assisted by the 8th Gurkhas on their left, while men of the 14th Punjab Regiment cut the southern approaches of the town. Indian mountain gunners provided deadly artillery support.

In one ambush the Punjabis trapped a Jap troop-carrying lorry. The entire load, comprising a Jap officer and 12 other ranks, were killed. An animal-transport NCO, Havildar Prab Dyal, from Kangra, accounted for eight of the casualties.

At this point the Division struck the Ye-U-Mandalay railway. Punjabis patrolling south of Budalin cleared

(Above) BUDALIN. Infantry assault into the flames.
(Below) MONYWA. Men of 9/14 Punjab and 9 (M.G.) Jat during attack.

---

several villages in a matter of a few days and were soon overlooking Monywa, an important railroad junction and once a flourishing Chindwin port.

For days the Punjabis advanced over flat country riddled with enemy bunkers and foxholes and captured an airfield at Alon, about 10 miles north of their prize objective, before setting siege to Monywa.

On the left of these troops, another brigade of the Division set out in a column from Ayadaw—the plan being

100 Brigade crossing the Irrawaddy. The Division dealt a crushing blow to the enemy here.

AIRSTRIKE on Payitkon and Kyehmon.

ROAD BLOCK on bridge is cleared during advance.

to sweep through the area bounded by the Mu River on the left and the Chindwin on the right and exterminate some Jap long-range penetration groups and suicide parties, the presence of which had become known from captured documents.

The final assault on Monywa started at mid-day. It was preceded by a heavy airstrike. Just before zero hour enemy positions were further pounded by British gunners.

The battalions which took part in this action were the

MONYWA. Sepoys of 9/14 Punjab search the gaol.

Northamptons—operating on the left flank—and the 14th Punjabis who launched the attack from the north and the 8th Gurkhas who cut escape routes to the south.

In the face of opposition from heavy bunker positions the British troops captured three objectives, Ledi, the rifle range and the hospital. The Punjabis' advance was seriously held up by automatic fire from concrete defences which commanded the road and the surrounding fields.

The final entry into the town was a great anti-climax to

MEN of 1 DEVONS move through Monywa.

---

the feverish tempo of fighting hardly two days before. Most of it was taken without exchange of a shot. The only opposition came from a few snipers in the extreme south of the town.

Starting soon after day-break men of the 14th Punjab Regiment who had suffered many casualties in their previous attempts to break the enemy resistance, were half way into the town before 10 a.m. The last of the enemy had been dealt with by noon.

BATTERED MONYWA. This was the main street.

Monywa was a mass of ruins. The high two-storied commercial buildings, the church and a gurdwara built by the Sikh community just before the war, all wore a look of desolation. The only signs of recent habitation were long slit-trenches and foxholes dug by Japs along the roads and in the compounds of bungalows.

One look at the enemy's main defences showed what the Punjabis had been up against when attacking the enemy earlier. Taking advantage of a high embankment run-

GUNNER signal party fix overhead cable.

RECCE PARTY of 9/14 Punjab pass newly-dug Japanese position.

ning at right angles to the river bank and the main road—erected by the Burmese to keep the Chindwin floods out and a good enough natural defence line—the Japs had prepared bunkers of stone and wood.

On the side facing the Punjabis the embankment wall was buttressed with heavy chunks of stone. All round the bunkers were bomb and shell craters but they had remained undamaged.

MYINMU AREA. Sepoy gazes on body of Burman mutilated by Japanese.

The advance up to Monywa was made by the 20th Indian Division without any armour support. As, however, the Division started fanning out south of Monywa—towards the triangle formed by the confluence of the rivers Chindwin and Irrawaddy—and also in the east where the Ayadaw column was now only a few miles north of the Irrawaddy—after combing through a large stretch of the Shwebo plain, armoured cars of the Indian Armoured Corps arrived and joined the fast moving Infantry.

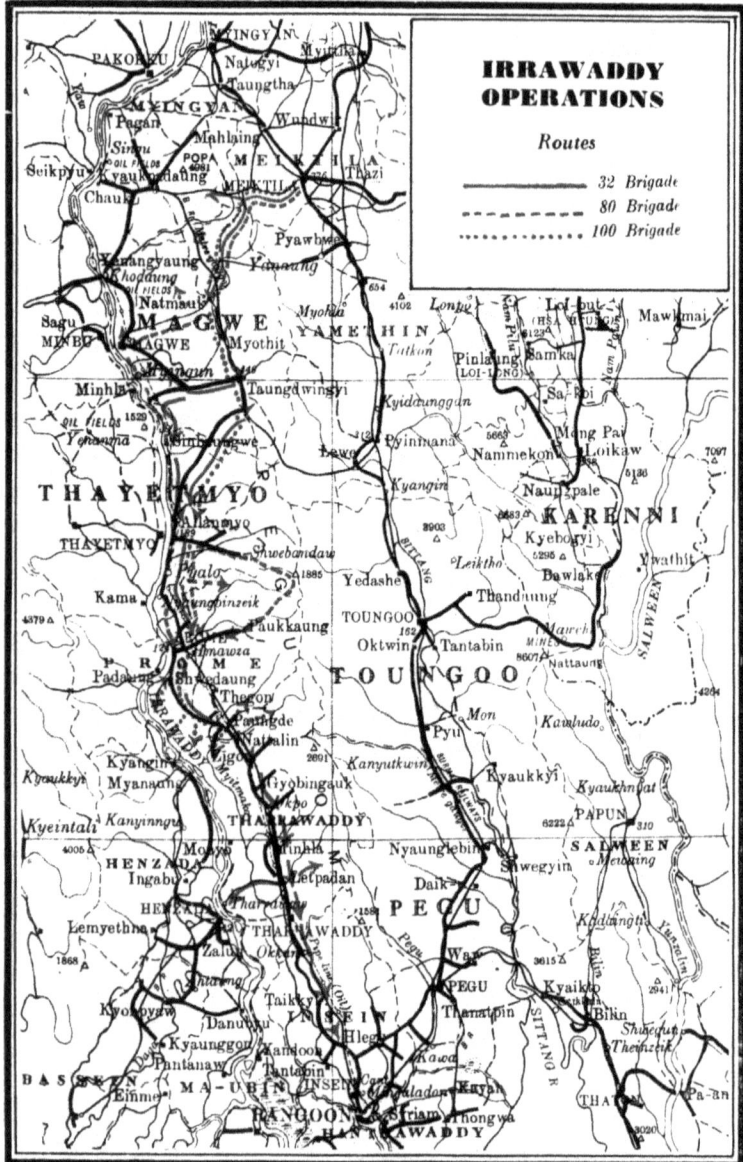

The stage was now set for the final spurt towards Mandalay, across the Irrawaddy. The troops in the Chindwin-Irrawaddy delta were ordered to draw and contain maximum enemy troops from the Myinmu area, from where the 20th Indian Division was shortly to push across the Irrawaddy.

The work done by men of the 12th Frontier Force Regiment and the 1st Gurkha Rifles in the delta area contributed substantially to the marked element of surprise when the blow was struck on the enemy.

Myinmu on the north bank of the Irrawaddy, where the river turns south before meeting the Chindwin, soon became the 20th Indian Division's main front.

The town was occupied after a sharp clash in which the enemy lost heavily in stores and equipment.

In a village near Myinmu, Gurkhas counted 82 Jap bodies after a two-day action. During the siege the enemy made several desperate attempts to escape across the river. The Gurkhas sank five large boats, carrying 25 men in each, and two small boats with the help of a machine gun battalion of the 9th Jat Regiment. The survivors were further plastered with automatic fire.

At one point the Gurkhas watched by moonlight 24 Japs jump into the river, all complete with arms and equipment, and perish one by one. Men of the 17th Dogra Regiment also contributed to the bag with a number of successful patrol clashes.

Armoured cars of the 11th (P. A. V. O.) Cavalry assisted the mopping-up operations in the widely scattered villages. In one encounter they killed seven Japs out of seven.

On the north bank of the Irrawaddy now while the 19th Indian Division was battling on its bridgehead at Kyaukmyaung, the 20th Indian Division was poised to strike a new blow which would break the Irrawaddy line.

To contain the 19th Division's bridgehead and at heavy cost, the Jap command had already committed maximum effort. The new bridgehead was to be a shrewd tactical blow which would further disorganise his defences and finally break his capacity to resist.

First the new bridgehead was to draw off more forces from the defence of Mandalay itself, second it was to help commit forces south of the river which would otherwise be employed in holding back the forthcoming blow from a new bridgehead at Pagan on the west towards Meiktila by 17 Indian Division And this later was to be the decisive strike which must at all costs succeed.

Although the 20 Division bridgehead played a subsidiary role in the overall tactical employment of the Fourteenth Army in this decisive battle of the Irrawaddy it was none the less important.

For the Division itself it proved to be its finest hour. In the bridgehead battle which lasted nearly a month before the break-out to the east began, the Division fought its most decisive action since the holding of the Shenam saddle. The first period was marked by bitter counter-attacks by the enemy repelled only by unsparing resistance of great ferocity by General Gracey's troops.

The crossing began on the night of February 12/13, the 13th Frontier Force Rifles and the Border Regiment forming the spearhead of the major crossing, while the Northamptons and the 14th Punjab established another bridgehead further west.

The operation was a tricky one. A high wind blew on the wide river and some of the crossing boats stuck in mid-stream on shifting sandbanks.

A heavy airstrike by Liberators and Lightnings two days before the assault crossing had liquidated gun positions from which the Jap had been harassing our troops on the northern bank.

The Japs were taken by surprise. The landing itself was unopposed. Before dawn came up, the Indian and British troops had time to dig in and consolidate a perimeter. Then the Japanese counter-attacks began. But in three days fighting the bridgehead was enlarged to three and half miles in length to a mile and a half in depth. The ground was firmly held.

IRRAWADDY. 14/13 F. F. Rif. land on South bank near Myinmu.

On the third day Jap aircraft appeared, and strafed the bridgehead area, and the same night the first determined enemy counter-attack came in. Not only was there fighting on land but Japs came down the river in boats and attempted to attack from the rear.

Fighting for the next five days was equally bitter with Indian troops on the western sector of the bridgehead suffering from most of the counter-attacks.

The Japs brought up armour in a vain attempt to

(*Above*) *IRRAWADDY CROSSING. Infantry of 14/13 F.F. Rif. climb aboard and ...*
(*Below*) *... cross in boats constructed by 481 Fd. Coy. I. E.*

regain ground but the majority of the tanks were knocked out by rocket-firing Hurricanes.

The twenty-second Indian V.C. of the war, and the Division's second, was won, in one of these actions, by Jem. Parkash Singh of the 13th Frontier Forces Rifles whose platoon bore the main weight of a night attack lasting over three hours. Flame throwers, artillery, mortars and medium machine guns were used in the attack. The platoon havildar and the

IRRAWADDY, South bank. Mortarmen offload bombs.

---

officer commanding were wounded. The Jemadar, though wounded himself, continued to direct the action, dragging himself forward on his hands and knees. He went forward to a two-inch mortar post and with his batman also wounded continued firing until the ammunition ran out. From dead and wounded he collected remaining ammunition and distributed it to his men. Finally he took over a Bren gun and was again wounded. Wounded a third time he stuck to his post and continued

"STEWART" tanks of 7 Cav. move on to the ferry near Myinmu.

to encourage his men. Finally he was wounded for a fourth time by a grenade burst and died shortly afterwards still in action after assuring his company commander that he could look after himself.

Nearly every unit of the Division had tales of valour to tell during this bridgehead fighting. Men of the 17th Dogras nipped in the bud an attempted long range penetration patrol when they ambushed a party of 40 Japs bathing in the river and killed the majority. A

THE FAR SIDE. They advance along a newly-built track.

---

party of the 8th Gurkha Rifles charged three 105 mm guns with drawn kukris while the guns were firing and decapitated the crews. Indian mountain gunners joined in by surprising a party of Japs at a meal and settling their fate with tommy guns and hand grenades.

Biggest individual slaughter was on the village of Talingon in early March, where after a week-long battle in which the prime participants were riflemen of the 10th Gurkhas, more than 500 Japs were killed. For five nights continuously the Gurkhas had been in contact with the enemy. A strong Jap company attacked two platoons of Gurkhas for over five hours and wave after wave was only beaten off after hand-to-hand fighting.

Then the break-out to the east began. While 19 Indian Division moved on to Mandalay from Madaya the 20th Division struck east towards the Jap escape routes.

The air was ours and Hurribombers were at call. Indian-manned tanks worked alongside the advancing Infantry. Sappers joined in with assault detachments to blow in bunkers with bee-hive charges.

Fighting in rocky undulating country interspersed with mango orchards and banana groves, the bridgehead troops forged ahead. A month after the crossing they had advanced twelve miles east towards Mandalay.

The historic town on the banks of the Irrawaddy with its fort which for so long defied us, had fallen. In Meiktila we were firmly established and the frantic Japanese attempts to take the town were costing them only more men, more guns, and more supplies.

South east of Mandalay the 20th Division swiftly captured Myotha on the Sagaing-Myingyan railway with the aid of armour and shortly afterwards cut the main Mandalay-Rangoon road at Bilin 26 miles south of the city.

Next objectives were Wundwin and Kyaukse. The object in the first case was to relieve hard-pressed 5 Corps in Meiktila. The move was brilliantly successful. 100 Brigade less a Bn. at Myotha, was strengthened by tanks, "Priests" and armoured cars; and swept down through Pyinzi and Pindale, covering the 81 miles to Wundwin in three days. The administrative area of the Japanese 18th Division was thrown into confusion, headquarters, depots and hospitals being overrun. Great quantities of M.T. and ammunition reserves were destroyed and much rolling stock, equipment and stores were captured. The force then moved north along the Rangoon-Mandalay road, to link up with 32 and 80 Brigades which had been engaged in bitter fighting in front of Kyaukse. The enemy's intention had been to withdraw his troops from Mandalay down the railway towards Rangoon, but 20 Division's rapid advance had forced them on to the rough tracks at the foot of the hills east of Kyaukse. 80 Brigade from the west and 32 Brigade from the south closed in steadily, supported by heavy air-strikes, until the Japanese position in the town became untenable. The remains of two divisions—the 15th and 31st—were forced into the Shan States and were useless to the Japs throughout the remainder of the Battle for Burma.

In the station wrecked by the R.A.F. air strikes stood a shattered evacuation train—the last train that never left. Its 23 wagons were loaded with medical stores, sewing machines, photographic material and a mass of magazines and books. The bodies of its intended passengers were scattered over the station yard.

The Japanese forces on the Irrawaddy had now beyond doubt been broken. The area between the river and Meiktila was cleared, road communication had been re-established from the north with the gallant 17 Division garrison.

The battle of the Irrawaddy was over. The 20th Division could now assess what new havoc it had wreaked amongst the enemy.

The toll of Japanese dead was at least 2,000 in the bridgehead battle and the eastwards break-out. In addition the Division had captured 50 guns including nine 105 mm., and thirteen medium machine guns. Sixteen tanks and more than 60 motor vehicles had been captured or destroyed. Summary execution had been done.

The Japanese powers of resistance had been destroyed. Out-fought, out-generalled, he had lost the decisive battle for Burma. His last natural line of defence had been broken. Before the eyes of the Fourteenth Army now was the glittering prize of Rangoon, the first city of Burma.

In his orders for the next advance—the thrust on Rangoon—General Gracey said, *"One day the phase we have passed through may be described as the 'defeat of an army'—the next phase will be 'the destruction of an army' "*.

32 and 100 Brigades continued to drive the enemy into the hills to the east of the road, until relieved by

elements of 36th Division. During the battle of Kyaukse the Divisional Reconnaissance Battalion at last arrived—the 4/2nd Gurkha Rifles—and after the battle the three British Infantry Battalions which had been with the Division since July 1942 were exchanged for the 2/8th Punjab and 1/19th Hyderabad and the 1/1st Gurkha Rifles, from 36th Division.

The next task set for the Division was to cut the enemy's communications to the oilfield areas and to seize Magwe. The advance from Kyaukse-Kume area started on 10th April. 32 Brigade led with light tanks and armoured cars, they moved across difficult tracks and very dry country, occupied Natmauk on 12th April, and Taungdwingyi on the 14th, thus not only cutting the eastward escape route from Yenangyaung, Popa and Magwe, but cutting the only M. T. road between these places and Prome. These moves came as a complete surprise to the enemy. Stops were put down on the road and river to the west of Taungdwingyi and took a heavy toll of enemy M. T. and river-craft. By marching and ferrying, 80 Brigade and 100 Brigade followed in that order, while a British Battalion—the 1st Bn. Northamptons, lent by 36th Division, blocked the Eastern escape routes of the enemy still resisting strongly in the Popa area.

At this period, the Division was joined by 254th Tank Brigade, less a squadron of "Lees" and a squadron of "Stewarts". 80 Brigade supported by 150 R.A.C. moved from Natmauk to Magwe, capturing Magwe with slight opposition on 19th April. Many hundreds of I.N.A. surrendered or were taken prisoner. Again, the capture of Magwe came as a complete surprise and many Japanese were killed withdrawing from Yenangyang without having the faintest idea that Magwe was in our hands. The effect of these operations and of 7th Division's drive from the north on the oilfields, was decisive.

That forced the enemy to evacuate the oilfields hurriedly, to abandon his M. T. and guns, and, what was much more serious for him, forced large numbers on to the west bank of the Irrawaddy. Those on the east bank broke up into small parties whose sole desire was to get away with-

TALINGON. 4/10 G. R. clear up in the burning village.

out being caught by our troops. The enemy's offensive spirit was completely broken.

The Division had concentrated by this time in the Magwe-Natmauk-Taungdwingyi triangle.

After clearing the main road for 15 miles south of Taungdwingyi, 32 Brigade handed over its transport to 100 Brigade who took up the chase supported by old friends, the 3rd Carbiniers. Strong rearguards were met 25 miles north of Allanmyo, and in the northern part of

Allanmyo. These were defeated with very heavy casualties to the enemy. More guns were captured and Allanmyo taken on 29th April.

At the Bwetgyi Chaung, 12 miles south of Allanmyo, strong resistance was again broken and a decisive defeat inflicted in which the enemy were very skilfully encircled. The advance to Prome 'was unopposed, and in spite of many destroyed bridges, Prome was entered with slight opposition on 2nd May, and Shwedaung 10 miles further south the next day.

32 Brigade concentrated forward close behind 100 Brigade, while 80 Brigade marched from Magwe to Allanmyo on the east bank of the Irrawaddy taking a heavy toll of Jap parties on the river, and on land, and capturing many more I. N. A. prisoners.

While 80 Brigade remained in the area north of Prome, and 100 Brigade in the Prome-Shwedaung area, 32 Brigade, again taking over the transport, tanks and armoured cars, advanced along the Prome-Rangoon road. They brushed aside any opposition with great elan, killing a lot of Japanese and capturing a great quantity of material, and equipment of all sorts. Considerable delay was caused however by the demolition of no less than 15 road bridges between Prome and Palon, 60 miles from Rangoon, where the foremost elements of the Brigade linked up with 71 Brigade of 26th Division on 15th May. Again the Japanese were completely surprised by the speed of the advance, and the bulk of 28th Army was either cut off on the west of the Irrawaddy or forced to retreat with little equipment and meagre supplies into the Pegu Yomas.

Meanwhile 80 Brigade were blocking a determined attempt by a strong Japanese Force to cross from the west bank of the Irrawaddy to Zalon, and to escape into the Pegu Yomas. Many casualties were inflicted on the enemy before, at the end of May, 80 Brigade handed over to 7th Division and moved south of Hmawbi. They left 2/8th Punjab, 1/19th Hyderabad and some of the Divisional Artillery under command of 33 Brigade and these only assisted in the final annihilation of this force.

BAILEY BRIDGE built by the Division's Sappers over the Nawin chaung 5 miles North of PROME.

100 Brigade also were busily engaged in preventing the Japanese from escaping from the west bank further south.

During June the Division took up its final positions along the main Rangoon road from Gyobingauk to Hmawbi (some 80 odd miles). Right up to V-J day, they were constantly hunting and harrying Japanese parties who were either trying to escape to the Yomas, or to eke out a precarious existence, once they got there, by raiding villages for food.

It was most gratifying to the Division to see Gen. Gracey officiating as 4 Corps Commander, helping to set the stage for the final liquidation of the Japanese break-out from the Pegu Yomas. Five battalions and a battery from 20th Division helped 17th and 19th Divisions in the actual slaughter. The following telegram received from Commander 4 Corps on 29th July rounds off fittingly the history of the 20th Division in the Battle of Burma. *"Extremely grateful for your unstinted help in loaning resources with which to consummate the destruction of Jap forces which you had so large a part in routing earlier in the shooting-match."*

In September 20 Division moved by air and sea, to French Indo-China, with the task of concentrating and disarming the 70,000 Japanese troops there, while General Gracey had the additional task of commanding the SACSEA Control Commission.

Its task there was considerably complicated by the lawless methods of the Annamite Independence movement, which gave it the additional and difficult task of preserving law and order until French troops were able to take over. 20 Division achieved its task with its usual quiet efficiency and its commander and "les Gurkhas", as the French called all Indian troops, won new laurels and many friends.

In December, 32 Brigade left for Borneo and 80 Brigade for Macassar in January, 1946, both in order to relieve the Australians in those places. Divisional HQ and 100 Brigade returned to Ranchi in February to disband. 32 Brigade returned and disbanded in June while 80 Brigade were due to do so shortly afterwards.

So a famous fighting formation has broken up but whether described as "a happy family" or "that band of happy vagabonds," its name and spirit will live on, and old members of all races and creeds including units attached at any time have a lasting bond between them.

THE   END

(Above) INTO PROME. Frontier Force patrol clears area near railway station.

(Below) SURRENDER in SAIGON. Jap officer surrenders sword to S. M. of 1/19 Hybad.

MORE FAMILIAR FACES.

Lt.-Col. E.C. ("Pick") PICKARD, D.S.O., Comd. 14/13 F. F. Rif.

Lt.-Col. ("Juan") HOBBS, D.S.O., Comd. 9/14 Punjab.

Lt.-Col. J. S. VICKERS, D.S.O., Comd, 4/10 G. R. examines a Japanese sword captured by one of his soldiers.

Sub. CHATTAR SINGH of 1/19 Hybad is presented with Japanese sword by Gen. Gracey.

Lt. Col. ("GUNGA") M. HAYAUD DIN, M.B.E., M.C. 9/12, F.F. Regt.

Sub. CHANDRA SINGH, I.D.S.M., of 1/19 Hybad.

Sub. Maj. (Hon. Lt.) AHMED KHAN, SARDAR BAHADUR, O.B.I., I.O.M., of 9/12 F.F. Regt.

During visit the Division, the C-in-C spoke with Sub. Maj. (Hon. Lt.) Mahbub Khan, Sardar Bahadur, O.B.I., of 9 Jat M.G. Bn., who has 31 years service.

HOMAGE TO A FALLEN COMRADE SEPOY OF 92 FD. COY. R. I. E.

INDIAN DIVISIONS WON A FINE REPUTATION IN WORLD WAR TWO

Field Marshal Auchinleck, Commander-in-Chief of the British Indian Army from 1942, asserted that the British "*couldn't have come through both wars (World War I and II) if they hadn't had the British Indian Army*". British Prime Minister Winston Churchill also paid tribute to "*the unsurpassed bravery of Indian soldiers and officers*".

Between 1945 and 1947, the Director of Public Relations, War Department, Government of India, published a series of short publications covering the individual histories of the WWII Indian Divisions. They followed a consistent format, having between 44 and 48 pages within illustrated soft card covers. They have an average of 50 monochrome photographic illustrations, and each has a full colour centrespread depicting a scene from the Division's wartime operations (drawn by official war artists). They were printed at various presses in Bombay and New Delhi, and each contains at least one map.

As condensed histories they are useful – particularly those which relate to Divisions for which no other record was ever produced.

The British Indian Army during World War II began the war, in 1939, numbering just under 200,000 men. By the end of the war, it had become the largest volunteer army in history, rising to over 2.5 million men in August 1945. Serving in divisions of infantry, armour and a fledgling airborne force, they fought on three continents: in Africa, Europe and Asia.

This Army fought in Ethiopia against the Italian Army, in Egypt, Libya, Tunisia and Algeria against both the Italian and German Army and, after the Italian surrender, against the German Army in Italy. However, the bulk of the British Indian Army was committed to fighting the Japanese Army, first during the British defeats in Malaya and the retreat from Burma to the Indian border; later, after resting and refitting for the victorious advance back into Burma, as part of the largest British Empire army ever formed. These campaigns cost the lives of over 87,000 Indian service- men, while another 34,354 were wounded, and 67,340 became prisoners of war. Their valour was recognised with the award of some 4,000 decorations, and 18 members of the British Indian Army were awarded the Victoria Cross or the George Cross.

RED EAGLES
The Story of the 4th Indian Division
9781474537520

During the Second World War, the 4th Indian Division was in the vanguard of nine campaigns in the Mediterranean theatre, Egypt, Eritrea, Syria, Tunisia, Italy and Greece. The 4th Division captured 150,000 prisoners and suffered 25,000 casualties, more than the strength of a whole division. It won over 1,000 honours and awards, which included four Victoria Crosses and three George Crosses. Field Marshal Lord Wavell wrote: "The fame of this Division will surely go down as one of the greatest fighting formations in military history."

THE FIGHTING FIFTH
History of the 5th Indian Division
9781474537513

As described in much greater detail in Anthony Brett James's book 'The Ball of Fire', the division saw active service in East Africa, North Africa and Burma.

GOLDEN ARROW
The Story of the 7th Indian Division
9781474537506

The role of this division is also duplicated by a much larger work: the book by Brig. M. R. Roberts. However, this booklet gives a good account of Kohima and Imphal and the crossing of the Irrawaddy. In 1945, the division was flown into Siam, so becoming the first Allied formation to re-enter South East Asia.

ONE MORE RIVER
The Story of the 8th Indian Division
Biferno, Trigno, Sangro, Moro, Rapido, Arno, Senio, Santerno, Po, Adige

9781474537490

The 8th Indian Division started its overseas service in the Middle East in the garrisoning of Iraq and then the invasion of Persia to secure the oil fields of the area for the Allies, before moving to Italy in 1943. Landing at Taranto, it pushed up the length of the peninsula in a series of major battles: breaking the Sangro Line, forcing the Rapido and turning the defences at Cassino, breaking the stubborn German resistance at Monte Grande and, finally, forcing the Po River. It won four VCs, 26 DSOs and 149 MCs along the way. During the war the 8th Indian Division sustained casualties totalling 2,012 dead, 8,189 wounded and 749 missing.

BLACK CAT DIVISION
17th Indian Division

9781474537483

This formation was committed to Burma from the early days when the British were in full flight from the invading Japanese. It remained in Burma right through to the end, when the starving remnants of the Japanese Army were making their own desperate retreat.

TIGER HEAD
The Story of the 26th Indian Division
Arakan, Ragoon

9781474537452

This is a history of the division said later by the Japanese to have been the opponent which they most feared. The 26th held the Allied monsoon line in the Arakan during two such seasons, repulsing every attack launched against it. Later it made a series of leap-frog landings down the coast to clinch the issue in the Arakan. It was the first division to enter Ragoon, invading the city from the sea.

A HAPPY FAMILY
The Story of the Twentieth Indian Division, April 1942-August 1945
9781474537476

One of the few Indian divisions in the 14th Army trained specifically for the war in Burma. Raised in Bangalore in 1942, it commenced active operations in late 1943 and served from Imphal through to the end. It established the 14th Army's first brigade-head across the Chindwin and its second such brigade-head across the Irrawaddy. Its final task was to round up the Japanese in French Indochina.

THE TWENTY THIRD INDIAN DIVISION
"The Fighting Cock Division"
Burma, Malaya, Java
9781474537469

The Fighting Cock Division is well recorded in the book by Doulton. This book gives coverage of the heavy fighting at the Kohima Battle, the capture of Tamu, the reoccupation of Malaya in August 1945, and then its strange role on the island of Java – concurrently disarming the Japanese garrison, fighting the insurgent Indonesian nationalists, and caring for 65,000 former internees pending the arrival of a new Dutch administration.

TEHERAN TO TRIESTE
The Story Of The Tenth Indian Division
9781783317028

This History deals with the 10th Indian Div's exploits in Iraq (under Maj Gen "Bill" Slim) its role in the Libyan battles leading up to El Alamein, the following two years of garrison duties in Cyprus and Syria, and finally, its fighting services in the Italian campaign (from Ortona onwards).

THE STORY OF THE 25th INDIAN DIVSION
The Arakan Campaign
9781783317585

Formed in Southern India in August 1942 for defence of that area in case of Japanese invasion, the "Ace of Spades" Division had its baptism of fire in Arakan in February 1944. It served throughout the remainder of that campaign the climax being the battle of Tamandu. Its victorious fight for the Kangaw roadblock was considered by many to have been the fiercest battle of the entire Burma war, while its liberation of Akyab was the first convincing proof to the rest of the world that the tide had turned against the Japanese.

DAGGER DIVISION
The Story Of The 19th Indian Division
9781783317035

Raised in the late 1941, the 19th was the first "standard" Indian Division. Its troops were the first to breach the Japanese defence line in Burma and to raise the flag at Fort Dufferin. It crossed the Chindwin in November 1944, driving on to Mandalay and Ragoon during seven months of continuous fighting. The 19th's exploits are graphically described also in John Masters' personal memoir, *The Road Past Mandalay*.

www.ingramcontent.com/pod-product-compliance
Lightning Source LLC
Chambersburg PA
CBHW041928090426
42743CB00021B/3473